365 CAREGIVING TIPS: PRACTICAL TIPS FROM EVERYDAY CAREGIVERS

CONTRIBUTORS:
PEGI FOULKROD, GINCY HEINS,
TRISH HUGHES KREIS,
RICHARD KREIS, KATHY LOWREY

COVER ART BY:
PEGI FOULKROD

Thank you buying our book! Caregivers need as much help and support as possible and, as caregivers ourselves, we want to share tips with others. This and other books can be purchased at RobertsSister.com.

Published by Robert's Sister Publishing, Sacramento, California

ISBN 978-1-329-75946-6

Thank you for your support!

Through everything, let there be love.

Table of Contents

Acknowledgements

This book could not exist without the generous spirit of caregivers. Caregivers not only care for loved ones and friends but also for each other.

These practical caregiving tips are our way of caring for other caregivers because we are all in this together.

Many thanks go to Pegi, Gincy, Richard and Kathy for their wisdom, their heart and their willingness to help ease the journey of other caregivers.

Introduction

After years of caregiving (too many to count between us!) and sharing tips, tricks, support, laughs and tears with one another we decided to share what we have learned with others.

These 365 tips have come from personal experience as caregivers and many are a result of lots of trial and error!

Some of these tips have previously been shared on our websites, through our social media platforms and on other caregiving related websites as well. We highly recommend the caregiving support site CareGiving.com (www.CareGiving.com) as well as Assisted Living Directory (www.Assisted-Living-Directory.com) both of which have a variety of resources and information for the caregiver.

We would also love to have you visit our own websites: Richard's website on chronic pain management (www.PickYourPain.org), Kathy's award-winning blog "Living with a Thief Named Lewy Body Dementia" (www.thieflewybodydementia.com), and Trish's website about caring for her brother with intractable epilepsy (www.RobertsSister.com).

By sharing our experiences through these tips, we hope your caregiving experience is made just a little easier.

GENERAL CAREGIVING TIPS

1. Create a one page summary sheet for your caree. Include: name, social security number, health insurance information, physicians and specialists, medications, diagnoses and caregiver contact info. Keep it updated and available to give to EMTs, emergency room personnel or just as a reference guide for you to use when contacting health professionals and medical supply companies.

2. Have a "go bag" for you and one for your caree. Contents for the caree can include: extra briefs, wipes, gloves, plastic trash bags, an extra set of clothes, extra reading glasses and pens as well as a light jacket.

3. Keep an extra copy of the summary sheet in your "go bag" and in your car.

4. Take the vitals of your caree daily. This will give you baseline information for blood pressure, pulse rate, oxygen level and temperature. This information will be invaluable when your caree is ill.

5. Be non-judgmental. This can be difficult when the caree is not caring for him/herself in the way you think is best.

6. Buy in bulk to save money. Does your caree easily break or lose their reading glasses? Buy several at a time online and have them ready to replace the lost or broken pair. (This does not apply to prescription glasses.)

7. Keep to a routine as much as possible. Changes in routine can be a seizure trigger or detrimental to the caree's health, as can lack of sleep. Having a regular routine will allow the caregiver and caree some semblance of order during a usually chaotic time.

8. Have "regular" clothes as well as "relaxing" or "I'm sick" clothes. Sweat pants and even hospital gowns are great alternatives during days the caree is feeling under the weather and may not have the energy to put on pants, shirt, shoes, etc.

9. Get a Durable Power of Attorney in place so you, as the caregiver, can talk to the doctors, hospital staff and social service agencies about your caree.

10. If your caree has difficulty with transitions, give lots of notice about upcoming appointments or activities and involve them in preparing for it. "Good morning! Today we have a doctor's appointment." "What would you like to talk to the doctor about today?" "We're almost to the doctor's office." "They are going to call you back soon to take your vitals." "We are waiting for the doctor in this room."

11. Reexamine routines. Sometimes it takes something major to shake up a routine (a doctor's order or a move) but it doesn't have to always be the trigger. We get into our routines and stick with them but being open to change can help all involved.

12. Caregiving requires lots of supplies. You might find it helpful to have a designated area for all supplies for easy retrieval when warranted as opposed to running around trying to gather supplies from different parts of the house.

13. Medical equipment can be a scary thing to young children. Talk about the items and how they work and if possible, let them experience some of them. Kathy says, "With my grandchildren, a drawer full of candy that they were allowed to choose from when they visited was strategically placed next to the hospital bed of my husband. In order to get a piece, they had to go into the room and ask him for a piece. The more they were exposed to the equipment, the less scary and confusing it was for them and the bond between the

children and their grandfather was not interrupted. Bribery can be a wonderful thing sometimes."

14. When going out, first do some recon and scope out restroom locations and if there are family friendly bathrooms. Taking care of your opposite sex caree or needing a large restroom due to medical equipment sometimes requires a family size restroom.

15. Trust your instincts. Is something not quite right with your caree? Investigate, watch them closely and take their vitals. Your instincts will be right!

16. Build a support network. Know who you can go to for help with your children or pets in an emergency, who is good at listening and who will research things for you.

17. Know when to say "No." Whether it's to social requests, volunteer opportunities, or family obligations, learn your limits.

18. Have food such as granola bars in the house so you can grab and toss them in your bag for doctor's appointments, errands, and other outings.

19. Compile a list of your caree's PCP and specialists, including their phone numbers.

20. Create a brief Medical History that lists known diagnosed diseases. List in chronological order all major surgeries and procedures and hospitalizations. Carry these lists with you in your purse or on a zip drive at all times. Be sure to keep this updated with any new medications or hospitalizations.

21. Compression socks are usually very difficult to put on your caree. Often the doctor will allow you to use ace bandages instead. They now make a self-adhesive ace bandage that does

not keep falling down. It grips like Velcro to itself and is washable and reusable. These are much easier to put on and maintain.

22. If using hospice, find out what services are available to you. You may not need them all right now, but you might be interested in one or more of them in the future.

23. Keep extra supplies on hand. Your caree might use disposable adult briefs, which you may get through hospice or have delivered to the house. Always make sure there is an extra package on hand. You never know when you will go through them faster than anticipated or when a delivery will be delayed.

24. If your caree has a life insurance policy, check the policy or talk to an agent. They may not have to pay premiums once they become disabled.

25. Go over all bills, files, insurance policies with the caree as soon as possible, particularly if they have always been the person in charge of the paperwork.

26. Take pictures or make videos. Life may not be picture perfect, but you will be grateful for those pictures of your caree with family and friends in the future.

27. Include yourself in the pictures!

28. Educate yourself on your caree's illness or condition. You are your caree's most important advocate and will often know more about it than the medical professionals you encounter because you are specialized in this. You definitely know more about your caree than others do.

29. Plan ahead. Know what might happen in the future or where to find the information when you need it.

30. Share with others. If you meet other people caring for someone with the same health issue, share information with them if you have it. You'll be able to learn from each other.

31. Keep an extra blanket or jacket in the car. It can be used by your caree as a pillow or blanket in the car, or taken into a chilly office so they can stay comfortable.

32. What type of music does your caree enjoy? Download it, find it on CDs, or make a list of where to find it so you have it available for their listening pleasure. Music is soothing and can calm down a person or help bolster their mood as well as distract them.

33. Check your community for free and inexpensive activities and events your caree might enjoy. Public libraries and senior centers have speakers who visit and give talks of one hour or less. The topics are varied and usually free.

34. Does the local community college have classes for seniors? These are inexpensive or free and cover art, exercise, music, yoga, and many other topics. See if you can enroll your caree, or if you and your caree can take a class together.

35. If you are not sure if a class will be appropriate for your caree, ask if you can attend for free once, or pay for just one visit rather than joining something that may not be beneficial.

36. If you find a class for one type of illness, such as a dance class for Parkinson's patients, and you think it would be beneficial for your caree even though they have another illness, e-mail or call and ask if you can try the class.

37. Do you feel like your brain is turning to mush? Check out free online classes on websites like Coursera or download an

app to help you learn a new language, play piano on an iPad, or learn a new recipe.

38. Medic Alert bracelets are a good investment for carees with memory or cognitive problems, epilepsy, chronic pain or heart conditions as well as many others.

39. The day or evening prior to any doctor's appointments, get organized. Print out the current list of medications, directions if needed, pack your bag with a snack, jacket, water bottle, book, paper, pens and your list of questions. Doing it the day before will save you from scrambling and stressing the day of the appointment.

40. Before leaving for a doctor's appointment, check the traffic. Do you need to leave earlier due to road construction or an accident? Have alternate routes in mind in case you have to change your route.

41. Allow plenty of time for the caree to get ready for a doctor's appointment. Know their routines: bathroom, snack or grooming routines all take time.

42. Know your caree's best time of day and plan accordingly. If they are at their best in the morning, schedule appointments for that time of day whenever possible.

43. If possible, try to combine something pleasant, such as lunch out, with something less pleasant, such as a doctor appointment. It will be nice for both of you to have something to look forward to after seeing the doctor.

44. Attend doctor appointments with your caree so there is another set of ears.

45. Prepare a list of questions/concerns before doctor appointments.

46. Take notes at the doctor appointments.

47. Keep a daily log making note of daily activities, mood and physical problems.

48. Take the log to doctor appointments as it may help explain a new behavior or health issue.

49. The morning of an appointment, call before going to pick them up in case they've overslept.

50. If the caree lives in a care facility, call the staff before arriving to be sure they have the caree up and ready to go.

51. When going out, what works best for you and your caree is the most important thing. If that means you have to leave an event early, do it and don't worry about it.

52. If possible, when you RSVP to an event, let the host know you may need to leave early and find out if it's okay. If it isn't, don't go – even if it is a family event.

53. Let the host know you may have to bring special food for your caree. You don't expect the host to provide it but give them a heads up there are diet restrictions so they are not offended when their food isn't eaten.

54. If you have a question, others have probably had it too. Don't hesitate to go on social media and post a question, especially if you're looking for a product that works or a solution to a problem.

55. Everyone needs something to do besides watch television. Try different things to find something that works to occupy your caree. Examples might be books, books on CD, puzzles,

word search puzzles, number puzzles, and listening to music. You can download things for free, borrow from others and find things at garage sales or resale shops. This is a great thing to ask others to help you with!

56. Use an electronic tablet for games or other programs to keep your caree entertained and interested during long waits.

57. Attend events and see distant family members without leaving home. Use FaceTime or Skype to attend a wedding, family gathering, or see family and friends at the holidays if you can't make the trip. It is a wonderful chance for you and your caree to be somewhere without the hassle. Yes, you'll miss the hugs, but it's better than missing everything.

58. Carry a pair of earplugs in case your caree is bothered by noise or an environment is too loud.

59. Another solution to being bothered by noise is to use ear buds and an iPod (or other electronic device) to listen to music or eBooks.

60. Make a copy of the front and back of your caree's insurance card and carry it in your wallet. You never know when you'll need that information.

61. It might be worth checking to see if you can have your caree's pet listed as a service companion. Service animals are allowed to visit nursing homes and other places such as rehab.

62. It's all in a name: Have your caree's name embroidered on the front of their shirts. If they happen to wander off or if your caree goes to day care or respite, or the time has come for them to move into a nursing facility this makes identification easier for those interacting with them.

63. Queen-sized sheets fit perfectly for the length on a hospital bed. Just tuck the excess under the mattress.

64. Whether the caree lives in his or her own home, a facility or has their own bedroom, put upcoming appointments on their own personal calendar.

65. Keep a supply of disinfectant wipes everywhere around the house. These are lifesavers!

66. For carees who do not like to put their hands in water, use a wet wipe to wash up. It can be much less bothersome than putting their hands under water.

67. Throw in a load of laundry at every opportunity.

68. Find a Day Program for your caree (check with Easter Seals and the Department of Aging for possible programs).

69. During back-to-school sales, stock up on office supplies. It's the best time to get a good price on folders, notebooks, pens, pencils, highlighters, glue sticks, tape, sticky notes, and printer paper.

70. We should all have emergency kits. Most insurance companies will not fill a prescription just so you can keep it with your emergency supplies but you can include the printed information that comes with the prescriptions in case you need to get an emergency refill.

71. If your caree uses any type of nonperishable supplies, including incontinence supplies, make sure to have these in the emergency kit.

72. If you have a question, ask another caregiver. Their situation may not be the same as yours, but they may have a suggestion that will work for you or will trigger an idea.

73. Is there something your caree likes to do such as watch movies or do jigsaw puzzles? If so, ask around and see if you can borrow them from others.

74. If your caree enjoys books, but you can't read to your caree as much as they'd like, see if your local public library has books on CD or pre-recorded books that you can borrow.

75. Use the DVR to record your caree's favorite programs.

76. If the doctor brings up the subject of hospice, there's a reason. Ask why it is being suggested. Don't be afraid of it. Hospice offers support to the entire family. Many supplies such as incontinence supplies, oxygen, a hospital bed, and durable medical equipment are covered by hospice.

77. Sometimes doctors do not suggest hospice even though it may be time to do so. As the caregiver, do not be afraid to ask the doctor if it is time to call hospice.

78. Check with your caree's insurance but in many cases you don't have to accept the hospice you are offered. You can do some research and select another one you prefer.

79. Even after hospice starts, you can request a different nurse or case-worker. Sometimes the fit is just not right and this is no time to settle for someone you are not comfortable with.

80. Plan ahead. Talk with the caree about their final wishes, including burial vs cremation and the type of service they prefer. Not everyone is open to discussing these things but try to broach the subject if possible.

81. Create an Advanced Directive in order to have a clear understanding of what type of medical assistance the caree would like at the end of their life.

82. Families are complicated. Keep everyone informed – even if it is just through an email because they have distanced themselves from the family.

83. Allow people to help even if it is not in the way you would do things. As long as it is not detrimental to the health of your loved one, allow people to do things in their own way.

MEDICATIONS

84. When picking up prescriptions, always check the medications before leaving the pharmacy. Are you expecting brand name but get generic instead? Check to be sure the medication looks like it is supposed to look (an extended release medication looks different than the delayed release). Check the dosage to be sure it is what the doctor had ordered.

85. Track all medications taken or used by your caree. Note the prescription number, who prescribed it, the intended use, cost, how many refills are left and any reactions to the medication.

86. Keep track of medications that are current but also those that have been discontinued. Make notes of any side-effects caused by the medications.

87. Use small, disposable medication cups when taking medications. This will help prevent dropping pills and searching for them!

88. Order the disposable medication cups online and buy in bulk – they are very cheap that way!

89. For those with swallow disorders give one to two pills at a time.

90. Create an Excel spreadsheet of all your caree's medications. One column for the medication name and dosage, next column for when it is taken and another column for any notes. Put the full name of the caree, the doctor and the last time updated at the top of the document. Also include allergies and sensitivities to medications in the notes section.

91. Set aside a specific day each week to fill the pill containers. Make notes of any issues. When you are done, place orders for those prescriptions that need refilling.

92. Use a marker to write the refill date on the top of the bottle cap. With one glance you can see when it is time for a refill.

93. Refill the pill containers during open pharmacy hours. This way, any problems with medications (such as you forgot to order a medication) can be handled immediately.

94. Build a rapport with the pharmacist – you may be a frequent visitor!

95. Ever had an issue with a pill cutter turning your pills into dust? Take a pair of tweezers and line up the score line on the pill with the pill cutters blade. No more dust.

96. Program the pharmacy's phone number into your phone. You will have the number when you need to ask a question about a prescription or need to reorder a medication.

97. As soon as you see you are running low on a prescription, contact the pharmacy for a renewal. They may need to order the item or contact the doctor for a renewal, so don't wait!

BATHING AND DRESSING

98. Install grab bars in the toilet and sink area of the bathroom before you even think you need them. By the time you do realize you need them, it will probably be because someone fell.

99. Install grab bars in the tub.

100. Install a sliding bathtub chair for those without a walk-in shower.

101. Use a shower chair for those who are a fall risk.

102. Bath rugs and mats are a tripping hazard. As pretty as they are, they may need to be removed from the bathroom (although be extra careful to keep the floor dry so no one slips).

103. People can be very sensitive to water temperature. Keep the water temperature as comfortable as possible for the caree.

104. Always check the water temperature before spraying it on your caree. Get to know the feel of the temperature that is most comfortable for him or her.

105. Using a spray nozzle on a shower can help direct the water as needed and keep it off of the person when they are shampooing their hair or washing up.

106. Use a "2 in 1" liquid soap so the same soap can be used to wash the hair and body.

107. Use a towel to protect privacy as much as possible.

108. Use a towel if the caree is prone to being cold while getting cleaned up.

109. Talk to the person when helping them bathe. Walk them through the bath ("I am going to shampoo your hair now" or "I am using the water to rinse you off now").

110. Use disposable wipes for cleaning up after using the restroom.

111. Read the package and know the difference between cloth wipes and flushable wipes. (If not, keep the plumber's number handy.)

112. Keep people independent as long as possible. Allow extra time for them to dress themselves and give encouragement.

113. Use disinfectant wipes to easily and quickly wipe down the toilet, sinks and counter after use.

114. Invest in an electric toothbrush to keep the caree independent and for healthy teeth and gums.

115. Use a clothing protector to protect clothes from toothpaste and other spills.

116. Let the caree use an electric razor if they want to continue shaving themselves but have a not-so-steady hand.

117. Keep nails trimmed so the caree does not inadvertently scratch themselves.

118. Become a self-taught hair stylist! Invest in a good pair of scissors or clippers so haircuts can be given at home. This will be helpful when going out becomes too difficult.

119. Buy slipper socks online and in bulk. Slippers can be a tripping hazard and the socks keep the caree's feet warm and on the ground!

120. Hospital-type gowns make wonderful pajamas, particularly for the incontinent caree who needs frequent changes.

121. Bedside, sink or "spit" baths are perfectly acceptable ways to help your caree get clean if your caree is having difficulties getting in a shower or tub. Consider handing a wet wash cloth to your caree so they can wash their face or hands while you are caring for other areas.

122. Keep supplies and grooming tools in the same place so both you and your caree know where to find them.

123. Inspect for sores, new moles, scratches or bruises while bathing the caree. This will alert you to any sleeping issues (such as moving around and bruising themselves), the beginnings of bedsores, etc.

124. Sometimes medications or incontinence can cause the body to smell. Body spray or the caree's favorite aftershave or cologne can make them smelling good again.

MEAL TIME

125. For the slow eaters, allow plenty of time to eat. Be prepared to prompt but not nag. The more time you allow for eating, the less stressful the meal will be.

126. Use colorful and original "clothing protectors." It will be much easier to get someone to wear something to protect their clothes from spills if it is in the caree's favorite color or has their favorite sports team logo on it.

127. Use dignified terms such as "clothing protector" instead of "bib."

128. Swallow disorders can be challenging. If a modified diet requires small bites, cut the food out of sight of the caree before presenting the food. This reduces any arguing about being able to eat larger bites.

129. Respect eating habits. Learn the difference between medically necessary and personal preference. Let the caree have some control over how they would like the food prepared, presented or eaten.

130. Sloppy eating, sniffling, coughing and burping can be things the caree cannot control during meal time but can be unappetizing for the caregiver to watch. Allow yourself to eat either in a different room or at a different time so you can also enjoy your meals.

131. For slow eaters, start the caree with the first course (fruit, salad) while you finish making the rest of the meal.

132. Use a straw if holding a glass is difficult for your caree. Use colorful straws, bendable straws, crazy straws – whatever helps make drinking an easier and more welcome activity.

133. Create smoothies that have a few fruits and veggies the caree will not or cannot eat with their meal.

134. Allow their favorite foods if possible. If they love ice cream but shouldn't have it daily, give a smaller scoop and serve it every other day.

135. Have easy "go to" recipes you, or someone else, can easily fix on those days you are too tired to invest in lengthy meal preparations.

136. When possible, make an extra amount of food while making one meal and freeze it for another night.

137. If three larger meals are difficult for your caree to consume, break meal times into several smaller meals throughout the day.

138. Try counting drinks (or bites) if the caree is balking at eating and drinking everything.

139. Be sure to ask the pharmacist if a medication should or should not be taken with a meal.

140. Use smaller plates if the caree is supposed to be on a diet but is resistant to it. If everyone at the table has the same size plate, smaller portions won't even be noticeable.

141. Involve the caree in the grocery shopping when possible. Even if they are in a wheelchair they might be able to hold one or two items (or a basket).

142. Does your caree love to cook but can't manage it on his or her own anymore? Involve them in the meal process: making a salad, dropping cookie dough onto a baking pan or stirring the mashed potatoes.

143. Have your caree share their favorite recipes. If writing is difficult for them have them use the computer or dictate the recipe to you so you can pass along to future generations.

144. When treating yourselves to a meal out, consider going at a time that will not be busy.

145. If you have the ability to go out to eat, do it as often as your finances allow. Find a restaurant that can accommodate your caree's needs and frequent it. When being seated, tell the hostess where you want to sit. Maybe you need to be closer to the restroom, or closer to the front exit. Maybe you need a larger table to accommodate a wheelchair or a quiet area. Explain up front you might be needy but they will be compensated. In doing so, the staff learns how to better serve you and your loved one making a more enjoyable evening for you both as well as an easy transition into the establishment for future visits.

146. Reconsider traditional meal times. Dinner at 6:30 may not be feasible any longer if the caree needs a lot of sleep. Consider an early dinner or late breakfast to accommodate changing sleep patterns.

MOBILITY AND MOVEMENT

147. If fine motor skills are declining, use Velcro button shirts and/or pants to keep them dressing independently for as long as possible.

148. Use elastic shoelaces so shoes can stay tied and the caree does not need to tie their shoes or be forced into a slip-on shoe they may not like.

149. If your caree has difficulty using a spoon, have dinner in a mug! Let them drink their dinner: soup from a cup.

150. Put a folding step stool in your car if the caree has trouble getting in and out of the car.

151. Fall proof your house (or the caree's house). Remove throw rugs, install grab bars (not just in the bathroom but in high-traffic areas of your home) and rearrange furniture so there is lots of clearance for walking with a walker or for a wheelchair.

152. Be careful if trying to catch the caree when they are falling. You need to make sure you do not also get hurt trying to prevent your loved one from falling. If you both go down that means two of you who may need care.

153. After a fall, check for injuries. If the caree is okay and able to get up, use a technique taught by Physical Therapists: have the caree turn over onto all fours and then "walk" themselves up by using a chair or some other stationary object to slowly get up on their knees. They can then get one leg under them, holding on to the chair or their walker. The caregiver is able to assist by keeping them balanced but is not hurting themselves trying to lift the caree.

154. If your caree is bedridden, use a wireless doorbell so they can contact you if they need help. Both the button and the bell run on batteries. Leave the button with them, and take the bell with you around the house.

155. An alternative is to use an old-fashioned bell they can ring to get your attention.

156. Loading a wheelchair into the car: fold the wheelchair in half with handles facing to the right. Hoist it into the trunk using the bottom of the trunk as leverage to help slide it in. (The handles will be the first part of the wheelchair in the trunk.) When removing from the trunk, again use the bottom of the trunk to "drop" the wheelchair back onto the ground. This requires the least amount of lifting which makes it easier on the caregiver.

157. When assisting a wheelchair bound caree in a transfer situation, lock the brakes and brace the chair using your body. If doing a side transfer, lean against the opposite side of the chair as many floor surfaces are more slippery than you expect and the wheelchair brakes will not be enough. If holding the chair from behind, brace your legs on the inside of the handle bars to steady the chair.

158. Some people can use a 4-wheel walker while others are better suited for a walker with two wheels. Consult the caree's Physical Therapist or doctor to see which is best for your caree.

INCONTINENCE

159. Incontinence can be difficult to manage but there are ways to make it easier. Use disposable bed pads or washable bed pads or even keep a supply of both on hand. There are days when these will be changed numerous times!

160. Recognizing incontinence is surprisingly difficult. No one wants to think their caree may have this problem and not many of us want to admit when we become incontinent. Watch for signs and then delicately bring up the subject of protective briefs or underwear with the caree.

161. If your incontinent caree needs to go to the hospital or an assisted living facility, communication is essential! It is important to let the staff know the caree is incontinent so they can properly manage it. They also should let you know if they notice an incontinent problem that perhaps you do not know about.

162. There are a variety of briefs out there. Some are pull up, there are varying degrees of absorbency (many are not nearly as absorbent as they should be) and some have closing tabs. It may be a matter of trial and error before you find the kind that works best for your caree.

163. A combination of briefs may be a solution. For instance, pull up briefs might be okay to wear during the day but the tabbed briefs are best used for overnight. As the incontinence worsens, these decisions will change.

164. Incontinence may not always worsen but sometimes it does. Be aware of the times there are leaks to see if there is a pattern which may necessitate the use of a different brief. (For instance, going to tabbed briefs during the day also.)

165. Urinal guards can be very helpful for men who no longer can stand while using the toilet. It is a guard that hooks on the front of the toilet and blocks any urine from spraying.

166. Use bed pads between the sheet layers as well as on top of the bed.

167. Use the bed pads for not only the bed but on other furniture and on the wheelchair as well.

168. If the caree goes to the emergency room, notify the hospital immediately of the incontinence. They have a variety of ways to manage incontinence one of which is a "condom catheter." This is not invasive like a traditional catheter but sits over the penis like a condom (hence, the name) and the urine goes into a bag.

169. Consider bringing in the really absorbent briefs from home when the caree is in the hospital. Hospital briefs tend to be flimsy and fill up quickly.

170. Timing of fluid intake can be helpful for overnight accidents. Be sure not to drastically limit fluids (you do not want your caree to become dehydrated) but time the intake of fluids to minimize overnight accidents.

171. Urine is very harsh on the skin. Use a barrier cream such as Desitin to keep skin healthy.

172. Use gloves when taking off the brief and when cleaning up the caree.

173. Use disinfectant wipes to clean the toilet and bathroom area.

174. Wash all bedding and clothes in hot water if urine has soaked through.

175. Minimize surprise or shock when the caree has an accident that is "new" (for instance, bowel incontinence overnight).

176. Treat the caree with respect when changing their brief. Explain what you are doing (I am wiping your bottom now; I am putting the brief on; I need to unbutton your shirt to get the brief on).

177. Pay attention to the staff of a Skilled Nursing Facility or hospital to be sure they are also treating the caree with respect when changing the briefs or cleaning up an accident. Report the person to their supervisor if they are not behaving respectfully. More training may be needed.

178. Medicaid helps pay for briefs, gloves and disposable pads. Have your caree's physician write a prescription for the supplies and contact a medical supply company that takes Medicaid.

179. Consider the caree's personal dignity when caring for them. Use the words "disposable undergarments" as opposed to diapers. Words can make a big difference in our caree's self-esteem especially when it seems they have lost so much due to ill health.

HOSPITAL STAYS and EMERGENCIES

180. Until things are settled at the hospital, consider being there at every shift change – especially if there complex medication schedules to be adhered to as any questions or mistakes can be caught early.

181. Include a tablet, a book and phone charger in your "go bag."

182. Appoint one person to communicate with everyone about what is going on.

183. Have an updated list of your caree's vaccinations and have it where you can access it, such as on your phone. If you are in the ER and are asked the date of your caree's last tetanus or flu shot, you will have the answer.

184. If you are going to the hospital for any reason, wear pants and take a jacket or sweater. Hospitals are cold!

185. Wear comfortable shoes – there is going to be a lot of walking involved!

186. A caregiver's list for the hospital should include, in addition to a list of the caree's medication, insurance information and doctor information, a bottle of water, a snack, cords for charging electronic devices, change for coffee, and a pad of paper and pen.

187. Keep cash on hand (including quarters) for snack machines when the cafeteria is closed.

188. Send a group text to concerned friends and family members to cut down on numerous phone calls.

189. If you can't be there during the doctor's rounds, have someone else be there to talk with the doctors. Ask a family

member or friend to visit at a time when you can't be there. A caree with cognitive impairment or who is very, very ill makes it difficult for them to give the hospital staff reliable information which could be detrimental to his or her health.

190. When talking with a 911 dispatcher, remain calm (it is a stressful situation but relaying information in a panicked state just compounds the situation). Give the operator information about what is happening and any chronic condition of your loved one.

191. Remember to eat and hydrate while your caree is in the hospital.

192. Know that the hospital staff and EMTs are on your side. Most (although maybe not all) doctors appreciate caregiver involvement.

193. Bring snacks;

194. Assemble a brightly colored folder or binder with copies of important information about your caree. For instance, his/her state issued ID (front and back), medical insurance card(s), list of basic information such as name, address and emergency contact information. Also include the caree's diagnosis and treating physician with the phone number, if your caree is a Veteran and even your caree's religious preference. Other information to include in the folder is whether your caree wears glasses or hearing aids, has mobility issues, needs assistance with transfers or if your caree has trouble understanding spoken words. Include the latest lab results, any surgeries in the past including cataract, allergies and a list of medications. Don't forget to include legal papers such as Power of Attorney, Advanced Directive, Physician signed DNR and Guardianship paperwork if applicable. Kathy says, "I kept a folder in an easy accessible area of the house and everyone knew where it was located in case of

emergency. I kept a second folder in my vehicle. The originals were in my purse."

195. Our smart phones have a list of contacts we store which includes a "favorites" list. At the top of that list, include "ICE" (In Case of Emergency). Designate who needs to be called if something happens to you.

196. Use your phone to take a photo of your loved one and identify them by their name as well as their condition and who should be contacted if something happens to YOU. Emergency personnel will know to check your home and then alert your "ICE" contact to check on your caree. Bonus Tip: Kathy has done this for her small dog as well. Kathy says, "If something happens to me someone will know to check on my pet."

ASSISTED LIVING or IN-HOME CARE SUPPORT

197. Enlist the support of other family members to help decide if additional in-home care is needed or if it is time to move your parent (or sibling or grandparent or other caree) into a care facility.

198. Each family is different but keep in mind offers of help may not come streaming in. Assign specific tasks to each family member willing to help.

199. If your loved one is currently in the hospital or a Skilled Nursing Facility, the placement counselors can help steer you in the right direction regarding permanent placement or provide information on in-home care.

200. Talk with your loved one's doctor to get his or her opinion on placement (although, keep in mind, their opinion does not matter more than yours). Think of them as an additional source of information.

201. Create a list of questions covering topics such as work history, skills and experience (both length of experience as well as experience with the particular needs of your caree) to be asked of potential caregivers.

202. Get a list of references for potential in-home caregivers or use a caregiving agency to do the interviews and reference checking for you.

203. Start with a screening interview with just you and the candidate.

204. After you have culled your pool of candidates, ask them back for a second (or even a third) interview. Include your loved one so you can observe the interaction between the two.

205. Get feedback from your loved one if possible once the interview has concluded and the candidate has left. If conversation is difficult, trust your instincts as to whether or not the candidate is the right fit.

206. Conduct a background check. Many of the agencies provide this service but request a copy of the background check so you can review it for yourself.

207. If your loved one is in an assisted living or residential facility, vary the days and time you visit. You don't want the staff to know you will always come at a specific time. You want to see what really happens, not what happens when the staff knows you are coming.

208. Get to know the staff where your loved one lives. There will be days you need to call and ask for their assistance, and you want to have developed a relationship so they know who you are and want to help you.

209. If you are looking for a facility where your loved one will be living, visit the one(s) you really like more than once. Visit at different times of day, try the food, and sit in on a class or activity so you can see how the staff treats the residents.

210. Educate the facility's staff on how your loved one likes to be addressed. Is it okay to call them by their first name, or do they prefer to be addressed only as Dr., Mr. or Mrs.?

211. When you get a call from the facility and they tell you your loved one doesn't have sheets, towels, a mattress pad, or something similar (even though you know they did have it), don't get mad – just get another one.

SHOW ME THE MONEY

212. In California, becoming a provider through In Home Supportive Services is one way to get paid as a caregiver. This is run through the county health services agency. If the caree is on Medicaid, contact the county to get the caree assessed for hours. The caregiver can then either hire a provider or sign up to be a provider themselves.

213. There are some states with a similar program but it is called a "Cash and Counseling" program. The caree has control over who they pay for services (such as an in-home assistant or family member providing the same service). Start with the Department of Health and Human Services in your state for that information.

214. There are waiver programs in many states that help pay for a stay in an assisted living facility. Again, the caree has to qualify for Medicaid before they can qualify for the waiver.

215. Personal Care Agreements are also a way to get paid by a family member. These are set up by the caree and the caree then uses their personal funds to pay for assistance. These are good if there could be family disagreements about one person doing the caregiving and not getting paid.

216. If the caree is a veteran, there is the VA's Aid & Attendance Pension Benefit program. Call 1.877.222.8387 for more info.

217. The Administration on Aging website (www.aoa.gov) is an additional resource with information about government programs and local agencies.

218. Information and explanations of Medicare benefits can be found at www.medicare.gov.

219. Social Security does not recognize Durable Power of Attorney so consider becoming a Representative Payee. This will enable you to handle Social Security benefits for your loved one and make changes on behalf of your loved one without making them endure an actual visit to the Social Security office.

220. A low-income caree may qualify for Medicaid benefits. These are different than Medicare benefits. Medicaid is administered by individual states but funded jointly through the Federal and State governments. It can be known under different names in different states (for instance, in California, it is known as "Medi-Cal"). Check with the Department of Health and Human Services in your state for more information.

221. Contact utility companies directly to inquire about programs geared toward helping low-income or disabled adults.

222. Additional local help can include home repair, assistance with utility payments and even legal services. Contact the local Community Services Agency to inquire about these assistance programs.

223. Agency resources such as local Regional Centers are another resource for the disabled. There are specific eligibility requirements so contact the local regional center in your area in order to see if your loved one qualifies.

ADVOCACY

224. Do not be afraid to speak up. You know your caree more than anyone. Speak up and advocate for your caree whether it is with doctors, nurses, medical supply companies or any social services agency.

225. Many social workers are doing their best trying to manage a heavy caseload which may result in subpar recommendations or a lack of attention to detail. Gently but relentlessly advocate for your caree.

226. Don't be afraid to fire your doctor or pharmacy! There are too many doctors and pharmacies to settle.

227. Acquaint yourself with the benefits available to the caree. People who are on Medicaid and are incontinent are eligible for a supply of briefs and bed pads, for instance. Health care providers do not always know this or mention this to the caregiver.

228. Appeal, appeal, appeal. Do not give up! Always ask for whatever has been denied to be reconsidered. Sometimes this will mean involving the doctor's office to help get an authorization or to write the prescription in a different way (for instance, saying it is "medically necessary.")

229. Write down your questions for your doctor as you think of them and clip them in the calendar by the date of the next appointment.

230. Keep notes for doctor appointments. We think we will remember everything but we can't. Having information written down means you can share it with health care providers when needed.

231. Be organized. Whether you file your papers in a filing cabinet, notebook, or some other system, have a way to organize your papers related to your caree. Worst case, have a bag or basket and dump all the papers related to your caregiving - prescriptions, receipts, notes, after visit summaries - in that one spot so you know where to find them when you need them until you can file the papers.

232. Educate Yourself. Learn as much as possible about your caree's condition so you feel confident enough to educate others and you are able to better advocate on your loved one's behalf.

233. Educate Others. Trish says, "When Robert meets a new doctor or other health care professional, I briefly explain what his seizures are like because most people equate "seizure" with convulsions and I don't want them to miss a seizure if they are looking for the wrong characteristic."

234. Take notes when in the hospital and emergency room. Trish says, "The notes I took while in the hospital actually once prevented Robert from being discharged too early. On the second or third night, the nurse had been inundated with patients and tasks and was unable to write her reports until the end of her shift. Because she had been overwhelmed, she neglected to accurately record Robert's vitals. I had diligently recorded his vitals each time they were taken and was able to show my notes to the doctors when they excitedly walked in talking about how Robert didn't have a fever the previous night. They quickly stopped talking about discharge once they saw my notes."

235. Create a medical information binder. Include all office visit summaries, lists of medications, contact information – anything that might be needed at the next visit or when seeing a different doctor.

236. Communicate. Ask for clarification from the doctor or nurse if you don't understand something. The patient needs an advocate to keep information flowing to and from the staff.

237. Don't be afraid to question. Doctors are very smart but so are you. You have knowledge about your caree - baseline behavior which is critical information to have.

TIME MANAGEMENT

238. Create a checklist of tasks you want to accomplish either that day or that week.

239. Use mail-order catalogs for supplies as much as possible. The ease of having supplies delivered versus battling traffic and crowds cannot be over-rated.

240. As you think of something someone else could do for you such as return library books, make a list of those things. When someone asks what they can do to help, refer to the list.

241. Do some tasks at night to help make the morning go quicker (set up the coffeemaker; make the lunch; set out clothes for the next day).

242. Time tasks. Give yourself 30 minutes to clean the bedroom and bathroom and stick to it. It may not be completely done in 30 minutes but it will be close.

243. When things seem too overwhelming set aside the non-essential tasks. These can wait until tomorrow.

HOLIDAYS

244. Plan far ahead for the holidays, especially if you want to change what your family has always done.

245. Do you want to get together with extended family for the holidays? Would you prefer to go to someone's house or be the host? Decide and let people know.

246. Let people know if there will be a change in the gift giving. Maybe it's no longer possible for you to buy gifts for the 12 family members you see at Christmas. Suggest a different plan as early as possible before people start their shopping. One suggestion might be that each person brings one $25 gift card, wrapped, and then you make a game out of picking the gift cards.

247. Start holiday cards early! Especially if your caree likes to send cards but is a slow writer. Give them extra time to complete the cards so there is less stress. Yes, start even before Thanksgiving!

248. Help the caree decorate their house. The decorating might be downsized but a few small decorations can lift a person's spirits during the holiday season.

249. For family gatherings, ask the caree to contribute something that will make them feel a part of the event but is not too taxing.

250. Help the caree choose the gifts they are giving to people. Maybe they need help shopping or deciding what to give or need guidance on how much to spend because they no longer can manage their finances. Let them enjoy the satisfaction of giving but in a way that works for both of you.

251. Involve the caree in decorating the house such as picking out the tree or hanging ornaments or lighting a candle. Even if they need help with their part or their contribution is small, it will help them feel involved in the holidays and help keep traditions alive.

252. Have a gift wrapping party. Have people over to help wrap presents (either yours or your carees).

253. Does your caree like music? Play holiday music as often as possible to get everyone in a festive mood.

254. Take advantage of downtime (or make time for downtime) and watch a traditional holiday classic with your caree. Who can resist Frosty the Snowman or It's a Wonderful Life?

255. When you are the hosting family for a party or family gathering, use disposable items such as plates, cutlery, napkins, tablecloths and glasses to cut down on your work and allow time to enjoy the party without dreading the clean up after.

TRAVEL

256. When packing for a caree who is incontinent, pack one suitcase with disposable pads, gloves, briefs, wipes and large garbage bags.

257. There will be room for the dirty laundry as the suitcase empties of the disposable materials. Use the large garbage bags for any soiled or wet clothing items. Bonus tip: buy scented garbage bags!

258. Hotel garbage cans are small so also use the larger garbage bags to dispose of the used incontinent materials.

259. Before leaving on the trip, find the closest pharmacy or drugstore and put the address, phone number and hours they are open on the itinerary. You never know when you might run out of briefs, bandages, wipes or some other caregiving necessity.

260. It might be necessary to fill a controlled medication while on vacation. Prepare for this contingency by checking when the refill date will be and if the medication can be filled early. If not, find a pharmacy in the area to refill the medication.

261. You want to take enough medications for you for every day of the trip plus enough for a few extra days in case you are delayed or any pills are dropped and can't be recovered. Your pharmacy may be able to get a vacation allowance which will let them fill prescriptions early.

262. Know that if the medication needs to be refilled at a different pharmacy, all the refills currently available will be lost. A new prescription will need to be sent to the usual pharmacy when you return from vacation.

263. When you travel, unless you are going somewhere remote, remember that as long as you have the medications with you, you can buy almost anything else you need.

264. Incontinent or not, pack one to two big, black plastic garbage bags to put dirty clothes in while traveling.

265. When staying at hotels, try to stay at one that offers a free breakfast. It will make the morning go smoother if you don't have to rush out to find a place to eat.

266. Notify the airline when purchasing tickets if the caree will have their own wheelchair or if they will need additional assistance.

267. Get to the airport extra early. With wheelchairs or medications being carried on there will be a delay. Get to the airport early knowing going through security will take an extra amount of time. Then treat yourself and your caree to lunch or relax before the flight with a good book.

268. Consider getting a portable door alarm to take with you on a trip. If your caree opens the door to the room during the night while heading to the bathroom, you'll be awakened and able to point them back into the room.

269. If your caree is the opposite sex, before sending them into the bathroom in an airport, assess the situation. Sometimes bathrooms will have doors leading into two corridors, easily confusing someone. Look for a family bathroom instead because it will have only one door. They can still go in alone, and you can stand outside and wait for them.

270. Never put medications into the checked luggage when you travel. Always carry the medications needed for the duration of the trip, plus extra, onto the plane with you. Fill the weekly containers, and take extra pills in the original bottles, with

paperwork from the pharmacy. Put it all into a gallon Ziplock bag and carry it in your carry-on so you can answer any questions and keep the medications safe.

271. Take a copy of every prescription, the phone numbers for the doctor and pharmacy, and your prescription chart (if you have one). Gincy says, " If there is a problem, my husband can breeze through security and I can explain the situation to the TSA agent."

272. When at the hotel, use the in-room safe to store the medications. You will always take the day's supply with you but keeping the rest of the medication in the locked safe will provide peace of mind and save you from carrying a week's worth during the day's activity.

273. If your caree has trouble walking any distance, ask for a wheelchair in the airport or a ride to the gate.

274. When you arrive at the gate, ask for pre-boarding if it is possible.

275. Remember your caree's limitations when you travel. They may have been able to go all day every day before, but now they need to rest every day. If they have to rest at home, they will need to rest on vacation.

276. Schedule downtime after a travel day. Plan for rest and recovery periods during the trip.

277. Stick to a routine as much as possible. Filling up the itinerary with activities is not feasible when traveling with your caree. If the caree usually goes to bed early and sleeps in, it might be best to stick to this schedule while on vacation. Vacation is a break in routine but too much of a disruption may be detrimental to the caree.

278. Temperature changes can cause chronic pain to spike. Bring warm/cool clothing when possible.

279. Carry travel ice packs or heat packs for those with chronic pain. Alternatively, carry large Ziplock bags and refill with ice at gas stations or at the hotel.

280. Take inexpensive night lights with you when you travel. Use them to light the path to the bathroom. Since they are inexpensive, it won't matter if you forget them.

281. Splurge and purchase a night light/air freshener combo!

282. Bring along travel packs of hand wipes. Keep them in your bag or purse for accessibility at any time.

283. Bring extra briefs, gloves, wipes and garbage bags in the carry-on bag so they are accessible while in the airport or during day trips.

284. When you are at any event that is giving away free seven-day pill containers, take one every time! You'll never know when there's a weekend or overnight trip for which you need to separate out the pills that are taken two or three times a day. With these, you can write the correct time to take the pill on it with a marker (for instance, "Sat – AM") and then toss it out at the end of the trip.

285. Consider buying trip insurance. Respite care sometimes falls through or our caree ends up in the hospital before vacation. If a trip needs to be postponed or cancelled at least the insurance will help soften the blow.

286. Don't be afraid to borrow or rent a wheelchair. Before traveling, find out what assistance is available during the trip. Airports usually have free wheelchairs plus you can usually get a ride from the person driving the transport cart if there

are mobility issues. Consider renting a motorized scooter for those able to drive one. Sometimes you can arrange to have the medical supply company even deliver one to your hotel once you arrive.

287. Take advantage of the assistance that is offered. If you are flying and your caree has a difficult time, moves slower than most people, or is thrown off by noise or crowds, make sure you board the plane when they allow on anyone needing assistance. When you arrive at the gate, get your caree settled into a chair and talk to the person working at the counter so you can let them know you will be boarding early. Not every need for assistance is obvious, so this will give you time to answer any questions they might have.

288. Take a break from each other. Vacations mean close quarters! Whether in a car, plane or hotel room, sometimes people need a little break from each other. If the caree will be safe, let your caree stay behind in the hotel room and take a nap while you get out. If your caree cannot be left alone, try to book a hotel room that is more of a mini-suite with a bedroom and living area. Your caree can relax in the bedroom while you enjoy some time by yourself in the other part of your hotel room. Or, find one that has a small patio attached so there is a little extra breathing room.

289. Find a way to take a break whether it is with your caree or not. Yes, we are talking about respite! Whether it is for two days or a week or two, it will rejuvenate you in ways you never imagined. A change of scenery is good for everyone!

290. Be flexible with respite days. It is sometimes easier to find a respite facility if there are several dates to choose from.

291. When planning a respite, finding help for your caree can be a challenge. Kathy, who cared for her Hubby, used the resources at the Veteran's Administration to give her an

annual break. Trish uses the local Regional Center servicing her brother to help find respite care.

292. When taking respite, pre-planning is critical. Appoint another family member as a contact person in case you are unable to be reached during an emergency. Explain to your caree where you will be and how long you will be gone.

293. Give replacement caregivers plenty of notice.

294. Meet with replacement caregivers or take a tour of the respite facility. Both you and your caree will feel more comfortable if the caregivers and care facility have been checked out.

295. More on medications! Count and recount medications. Be sure there is enough medication for the caree if you are leaving him/her for a respite.

296. Create a "Get to Know (insert Caree's name)" document for the replacement caregiver. Giving the replacement caregiver information about the caree (quirks, preferences, food restrictions) will reduce or eliminate any surprises or problems.

297. Schedule meetings and doctor appointments around the vacation. Allow some leeway in case there are last minute preparations before the trip or a delay in returning home after the vacation.

298. Prepare the caree for your time away. Advise the caree of your upcoming respite time but be aware of how much time is too much to give them – you don't want them to become unnecessarily anxious.

299. Write the upcoming dates of vacation or respite on the caree's calendar.

300. Stock up on familiar supplies whether going on a vacation with the caree or during respite. Using the same brand toothpaste or soap can be surprisingly reassuring.

301. Ease into the return from vacation or respite. Allow an extra day or two to settle into the normal routine without planning extra activities once you have returned home. Working caregivers might even want to take an extra day or two off before returning to work.

SELF-CARE

302. Cheer your small successes! Did you finally get through to the medical supply company after the 100th try? Yay! That is progress.

303. Let yourself enjoy the downtime. Caregivers are on high alert so often that when there is a lull between emergencies we don't know what to do. Allow yourself a minute to relax, read or just feel content.

304. Make your own do-overs. If the day did not start out right (you lost your patience, things are not going your way), call a "do-over" and do just that. Give yourself permission to start anew.

305. Be gentle with yourself – do not be tempted to kick yourself because the laundry didn't get done or the house isn't dusted. Tomorrow is a new day!

306. When you feel stressed, breathe. Chances are you have been holding your breath or breathing shallowly without realizing it.

307. Think of "Take care of yourself" as the simple things - brush your teeth, drink water, eat healthy. It's not the big things like taking a day off for the spa that will make a difference, but the small, daily things that will make you feel more in control.

308. Take a break when you get information overload (and you will). There will be times where you can't read or hear one more thing about your caree's illness. Take that break and don't feel guilty about it.

309. Join an online support group for caregivers.

310. Do yoga at home or go to a yoga class.

311. Practice meditation.

312. It is always in the best interest of the caregiver to have a stash of your favorite candy kept in a secret place for emotional emergencies.

313. Accentuate the Positive. Find one positive thing in the day and write it on the calendar. Here's the catch: try not to use the same thing twice. It can be anything from the coffee was hot to my loved one remembered my name today. The possibilities are endless, you just have to diligently look for them and eventually you will be surprised at all the things that can make you smile, feel good, laugh or bring you comfort, peace or just contentment. It is often too easy to focus on the negative especially during caregiving so train your brain for the good.

WOUND AND SKIN CARE

314. The most important job in any wound care is to prevent infection - infections can slow a wound's healing process and various infections can also be life-threatening.

315. Create a "Wound Care First Aid Kit" which starts with a case or container. Sometimes these can be free with a purchase at certain drug stores.

316. If the kit is for a child's wound try using a Super Hero lunch box to hold everything.

317. Contents of the kit can include, gauze pads, Q-tips, paper or nylon tape, ace wrap, scissors, tweezers, Desitin, antibiotic cream, Vaseline, first aid gloves and small and large bandages.

318. Other items which may be needed are ice packs (keep in the freezer or use the disposable kind) and saline solution which should be kept refrigerated.

319. The first thing to do before dealing with any wound is to clean your hands. If this is an emergency situation and washing your hands is impossible, do what you can to clean the wound and then clean and dress the wound again once in a more sanitary situation.

320. After cleaning your hands, clean the wound using a saline solution, distilled water or even basic bottle water to rinse off the wound. This also helps if you are trying to remove a gauze bandage that is clinging to the wound.

321. Once the old bandage has been removed, "prepare" the wound. To do this take some gauze and gently remove any foreign debris, creams, etc.

322. Dry off any excess fluids such as blood, puss, etc. using gauze pads or any clean, non-lint fabric. Do not use cotton as it will leave fibers in the wound.

323. Before covering the wound, be sure to note any changes in the size and location of the wound so it can be reported to the doctor. Of course, also note if there is any discharge coming from the wound.

324. For a larger scrape, cut or worse surround the area with a small line of Desitin or similar cream before covering the wound. This will create a barrier around the area keeping dust and debris from entering the area once you put on the covering.

325. Use a healing cream such as MediHoney (which is available at the pharmacy) or an antibiotic cream. Be sure to check with the doctor to see which he or she recommends to promote the quickest healing.

326. Cover the wound with a gauze pad and use a gauze wrap or even an Ace Bandage to hold it on.

327. There is a way to wrap your leg with an Ace Bandage or other wrap to keep it on. Starting with your foot, raise your toes to the ceiling and wrap your foot in a figure eight design. Then as you move up to your ankle with the leg wrap, you need to wrap the bottom of your leg (your ankle area) tight and then wrap it looser as you move up the leg. This ensures that fluids do not puddle in your foot and that they are pushed back up and out of the leg.

328. Larger wounds will heal faster if you elevate the body part with the wound above heart level. This keeps fluids from pressing on the wound site and not allowing it to heal properly. The more often and the longer you can do so, the better.

329. To keep a wound from getting wet during a shower, cover the arm or leg only with a kitchen/lawn garbage bag, then pull a large rubber band up to the top of the bag to seal out water. This is only meant to be done for a few minutes (for instance, the length of a shower).

330. Wash the wound at least once a day with plain water or a mild cleanser (unless the doctor instructed you not to get the wound wet).

331. Soaking can help remove scabs and dead skin. This should not be done if the wound is deep.

332. A product such as Vaseline can also be used to loosen or remove a scab if needed. This also helps keep the skin moist and will help prevent bandages from sticking to the wound area.

333. Need a homemade Saline Solution? It's easy and cheap!
    a. Get a 32 oz mason jar;
    b. Run it through the dishwasher, to sterilize it;
    c. In a saucepan over medium heat, add 4 cups of distilled water and 2 teaspoons of everyday salt;
    d. Stir until all the salt has dissolved;
    e. Let the solution cool;
    f. Once cool, pour into the mason jar;
    g. Label the lid or mason jar and store in the refrigerator.

PULMONARY HEALTH

334. Tricks to loosen congestion: hot sprite, hot tea, hot lemonade - lots of fluids!

335. Increasing liquids helps to thin out the mucus;

336. Use a neti-pot to drain sinuses. This can be difficult to use for some carees so they may need some assistance.

337. Check with the doctor to see if a decongestant (and which kind) can be helpful.

338. Use foam wedges on the bed to prop up the caree's head and even their feet. If you have a hospital bed, use it to adjust the head and feet so the head is propped up to help during coughing fits.

339. Sometimes we have to deal with the gross stuff. Checking the color of the mucus coughed up can help the doctor diagnose an infection. Trish says, "Definitely not a fun job but I am very happy when I don't see any yellow or green in Robert's spit-up bowl. Although, imagine my initial panic when I saw brown but then remembered the Thin Mints I let him have an hour earlier."

340. If your caree can tolerate spicy foods, try having salsa and chips for a snack so the sinuses drain!

341. For those with serious and ongoing pulmonary problems, ask the doctor if a nebulizer would be helpful. If so, get a prescription for one to keep at the house when needed.

342. Ask the pulmonary doctor if an Acapella is an appropriate device for your caree. It is easy to use and can help loosen up chest congestion. It is a very simple device the caree blows

into to make it whistle. This surprisingly low-tech technique will encourage coughing.

343. There are two kinds of Acapella (one is blue, the other is green) so ask the doctor which is the appropriate one for the caree.

344. Ask the pulmonary doctor or advise nurse for any other ideas for pulmonary health. They may not tell you unless asked.

345. If an oxygen machine is used, be sure to have the medical supply company service it regularly (they recommend once per year but more often if needed).

346. Check and clean the oxygen machine filter in order to keep it dust-free.

347. Keep dust and pet hair to a minimum: either hire a housekeeper or dust and sweep frequently.

CHRONIC PAIN MANAGEMENT

348. Encourage the caree to live life but pace themselves. There may be projects that they want to complete but it is ultimately their decision to do as much (or as little) as they can.

349. A person with chronic pain might need to spread the tasks out over a longer period of time. More breaks (even if they are day long breaks) will be helpful.

350. Keep a log. Include activities, pain level and mood. This will help the caree, their doctor and you, as the caregiver, recognize reasons for increased pain or a possible medication problem.

351. The caree can use a tennis ball to press between the pained area and the wall.

352. Treat yourself and the chronic pain sufferer to a massage. It will not provide permanent relief but it will help temporarily.

353. You might need to try various therapies repeatedly before they work. (Medications, acupuncture, massage, TINS unit, etc.).

354. Don't take personally facial expressions or noises from the caree. Sometimes, the pain has a mind of its own.

355. Research Pain Management doctors and clinics. Set up appointments with each one and "interview" them. Take a list of questions and after all the meetings, decide which is the best fit for you and your caree.

356. Questions to ask the doctor include: How long have they been providing pain management care? Will patients see the doctor or the physician's assistant? Has the doctor personally

experienced chronic pain? What techniques, medications and devices are used?

357. Do what you can to make things a little easier for the caree. Get a 4-wheel dolly. The person in pain will be able to use it to continue to do things they did pre-pain (like taking a laundry basket to the laundry room).

358. Here is another quick recipe – one for a homemade ice pack.

    a. Gather a bottle of rubbing alcohol and two gallon-size Ziploc storage bags;
    b. Place one Ziploc inside the other;
    c. Pour equal amounts of rubbing alcohol and water into the inner Ziploc bag;
    d. Seal both bags then shake it up;
    e. After shaking, place it in the freezer;
    f. Your new ice pack will freeze but will not freeze solid allowing the ice pack to form and mold around wherever it's needed. When done using it, just refreeze!

ALZHEIMER'S DISEASE and LEWY BODY DEMENTIA

359. Call the Alzheimer's Association 24/7 Helpline: 1-800-272-3900.

360. Consider scaling back holiday activities. Too many people at once or home changes such as new decorations can have an unsettling effect on our loved ones especially if they are experiencing hallucinations.

361. Use your smart phone to take a video of your loved one on a good day. Tell them you love them and document their reply. Take photos. They don't have to be always smiling people, just every day occurrences like them watching television or interacting with someone. Even just a photo of your hands as they hold yours. You won't regret it.

362. Do not take anything personally. These diseases can be brutal and sometimes those with them can say things they would not otherwise say. As difficult as it may be, do not take these comments personally.

363. Find a neurologist you and your caree are comfortable with. As the caregiver, you will be relaying quite a bit of information to the doctor – sometimes things the caree does not recall or disagrees with – and a good rapport with the neurologist will help during these appointments.

364. If your loved one has a memory or cognitive problem, look into the Medic Alert Safe Return program which includes a Medic Alert bracelet for the memory impaired individual and their caregiver.

FINAL TIP

365. Remember that miracles happen every day.

CONTRIBUTORS

About Pegi Foulkrod

 Pegi is a recent retiree and caregiver to her husband. She is currently reconnecting with some of the activities she enjoyed in her younger years: art, piano and writing. Growing up and growing old with her husband, son, granddaughter and siblings, she is one of six children born to extraordinary parents in the late forties.

Her family has always been close and Pegi was taught from a young age the value of spending time together. It was not unusual to find them all around the kitchen table playing cards in the evening as young adults or as adults all vacationing together with their respective children.

She and all of her siblings were blessed to have their much cherished mother with them for 104 years.

Pegi blogs about her caregiving experiences at CareGiving.com and has contributed to the *CareGifters* Book Series.

About Gincy Heins

 Gincy is a teacher, author and volunteer as well as caregiver and advocate for her husband who was diagnosed with mild cognitive impairment when he was 55.

Gincy teaches classes for seniors in senior centers and residential facilities. She volunteers for the Alzheimer's Association, manning their table at health fairs and other events. She also holds writing classes for early stage Alzheimer's patients and their care partners for the Alzheimer's Association.

Gincy co-authored the book *After the Diagnosis,* has contributed to the *CareGifters* Book Series, and recently helped her husband write the chapter, *Steve's Story: Living with Mild Cognitive Impairment* in the book *Psychosocial Studies of the Individual's Changing Perspectives in Alzheimer's Disease* (Dick-Muehlke, Li, and Orleans). Gincy wants to give a TEDx Talk and is in the beginning stages of her latest idea: getting cards and cupcakes to caregivers so they aren't forgotten on their birthday. Gincy and her husband are the proud parents of one son.

You can connect with Gincy on Facebook (G-j Heins), Twitter (@gjandfamily) and Instagram (picsbymom).

About Trish Hughes Kreis

 Trish is a freelance writer and full-time Legal Administrator who advocates for her disabled youngest brother, Robert, in order to keep him as healthy and happy as possible.

Robert has lived with intractable epilepsy his entire life and lives with Trish and her husband, Richard. Even though Robert now needs full-time assistance, he declares everything "excellent." Robert continues to teach everyone around him how powerful the "magic of excellent" can be.

Trish is an advocate for more research on the long-term effects of uncontrolled epilepsy as well as an advocate for expanding the definition of family to include sibling care under the California Family Rights Act and Family and Medical Leave Act.

Trish is the author of *Forever a Caregiver* and can be reached through her blog RobertsSister.com, Facebook (Trish Hughes Kreis or www.facebook.com/RobertsSister), Twitter (@RobertsSister1) or Instagram (RobertsSister).

About Richard Kreis

 Richard has always been a very active person both individually and with his family. Richard is the proud father of three great kids and husband to a very wonderful and supportive wife. Richard is a Trifecta caregiver to his mom, Carol, who has heart issues as well as for his brother-in-law, Robert, who has dealt with epilepsy his whole life.

Richard is also a full-time caree for himself because of his chronic back pain and other related issues caused by a drunk driver in early May 1993. In spite of his pain issues, Richard is working toward a degree in Psychology and recently became a Notary Public and Signing Agent.

Richard enjoys gardening, taking photos of animals and nature and can be followed at www.PickYourPain.org where he blogs about his caregiving and chronic pain issues as well as on Twitter (@kreisr1) or on Facebook.

About Kathy Lowrey

Kathy cared full-time for her husband, lovingly referred to as "Hubby" in her blog about living with, caring for and loving someone with Lewy Body dementia, after he was diagnosed in October 2007 until he passed away in February 2014. Kathy's blog is honest, raw and sometimes hilarious because face it, sometimes dementia can be funny. Kathy is just a woman who loves her husband deeply and wanted to provide him with the best quality of life she could. Her faith is strong and her prayer through it was and still is, "Lord, what am I learning from this? How can I use it to help someone else and to glorify You?"

Kathy's Blog, Living with a Thief Named Lewy Body Dementia (www.thieflewybodydementia.com), was chosen by Healthline as one of the 25 Best Alzheimer's Blogs of 2012 and 2014. It can also be found on CareGiving.com, an online support community for caregivers of all types. Kathy says, "If the blog helps even one person find comfort or education I will feel like it was a success."

These days, Kathy can still be found in a caregiving role as she co-cares for her husband's 67 year old brother born with Down syndrome. She also works and volunteers at Habitat for Humanity and loves spending any time with her eight grandsons.